WOMEN IN THE CHURCH

Dennis R. Kuhns

Introduction by
Beulah Kauffman

Focal Pamphlet 28

HERALD PRESS
Scottdale, Pennsylvania
Kitchener, Ontario
1978

WOMEN IN THE CHURCH

Copyright © 1978 by Herald Press, Scottdale, Pa. 15683
    Published simultaneously in Canada by Herald Press,
    Kitchener, Ont. N2G 4M5
Library of Congress Catalog Card Number: 78-53968
International Standard Book Number: 0-8361-1852-9
Printed in the United States of America
Design: Alice B. Shetler

10 9 8 7 6 5 4 3 2 1

To My Wife and Dearest Friend,
JOYCE

CONTENTS

AUTHOR'S PREFACE

This book is an attempt to clarify my own thinking on the changing role of women in the church. It started as my mind warmed to the discussion that surrounded the adoption of the Mennonite Church study document, "Role of Women in the Church" at Assembly '73. It reached skeleton form in a series of sermons given at the Sunnyside Mennonite Church in Conneaut Lake, Pennsylvania. The manuscript was "fleshed out" in the discussions that followed the sermon series. As a result of this process, my conviction has grown that the Apostle Paul's instructions to men and women were more a matter of the apostle's call to discipleship and his understanding of the church as the body of Christ than any "order of creation" or a carry-over of his rabbinic training.

To those who are conversant with the material already available, some of what I share will be familiar. However, as I develop my thesis, I hope to raise two points that I believe are crucial to the discussion in broader Christendom and for the Mennonite Church in particular. They are: (1) the implications of the Bible's teaching that the church is to be the body of Christ and that this body is to be visible wherever believers gather and (2) the implications of following our Lord's way of the cross in all human relations. For those in the Historic Peace Church traditions this point cannot be overlooked.

Much of the material on the changing role of women in the church, pro and con, refers to the church but does not deal adequately with the nature of the church, bringing that understanding to bear on the issue. Since much of the material is coming from sources other than the believers' church tradition and thus does not have a perspective of the visible community of the Spirit, this lack is understandable. But for those of us who do hold to a believers' church, this biblical concept must not be left on the sidelines.

The same is true of our understanding of following the Lord in the way of the cross in all human relations. Much of the material does not include this perspective either. For too long those of us in the Peace Church tradition ourselves have related the way of the cross only to war and have not applied it in our homes. This biblical perspective also must not be left on the sidelines.

My thanks to those who have shared with me in this pilgrimage. I am indebted to those who read my rough draft and offered helpful criticism. I especially thank my brothers and sisters in the faith here at Sunnyside. Without their questions and encouragement, I never would have begun this work. It is my prayer that this document will be a positive contribution to the discussion of the changing role of women in the church.

Dennis R. Kuhns
Conneaut Lake, Pennsylvania

INTRODUCTION

To have a young Mennonite pastor write on the subject of women in the church is indeed refreshing and helpful. His readiness to speak to this issue I think reflects the openness of a growing number of leadership persons in the church to deal seriously and responsibly with it.

The understandings shared by the author are uniquely strengthened since they grow out of his concept of the nature of the church as understood from the believers' church tradition, and his conviction that for all Christendom, and particularly for the Mennonite Church, it is crucial to keep in mind the implications of following Christ's way of the cross in all human relations.

The reader is aware from the start that the author has a high regard for Scripture. The basis for developing his thesis is a discussion of the nature of the church and the servanthood stance for all believers, which is particularly helpful in understanding the evidences of kingdom life that are to be resident and observable in each congregation. In the author's words, understanding the nature of the church "has profound implications for our discussion of the changing role of women in the church."

While much has been written about the place of women in the family, in church, and in society—a great deal of it helpful, some of it sub-Christian—by far the bulk of available literature on this subject has come from sources outside the believers' church tradition. Pastor Kuhns, writing out of the believers' church heritage, gives to us a resource that is tailor-made for the Mennonite constituency. He is one with his readers; he understands our roots and our almost five-century pilgrimage.

The author clearly and helpfully illustrates how the church has in many areas been shaped more by culture and society than by following Christ's example of self-giving love. This, he believes, has been true in our understanding of the role of women in the life of the church. On the basis of the true essence of the church, as described in Ephesians 2:14-16, the author calls his readers to a "more critical discernment of the traditional teaching on the role of women in the church." He cautions us to examine whether some of our teachings and practices reflect a hierarchical view of the church rather than a believers' church understanding of the nature of the church.

We are helpfully reminded by the author that to be united to Christ is to have the old order replaced with a new order (2 Corinthians 5:17). Pastor Kuhns has given a significant gift to the Mennonite Church in helping us to understand more clearly the meaning of the church and the implications that has for opening to women the full range of opportunities and responsibilities to which all members of the body of Christ are called.

Following the introduction at Assembly 73 of the study document, "Role of Women in the Church," a task force (four men and four women, appointed jointly by the Mennonite Board of Congregational Ministries [MBCM] and Women's Missionary and Service Commission) was asked to revise the study document. The revised document, "Women in the Church," was then circulated to all Mennonite congregations for study, action, and response.

At the request of MBCM, the task force prepared a proposed statement on this issue which was reviewed by the General Board prior to Assembly 75. Using the responses received from General Board members, the task force prepared the summary statement, "Facilitating Biblical Understandings Concerning Women and Men in the Church." This statement was then presented to Assembly 75 delegates for discussion. Following extended consideration, the statement was accepted by Mennonite General Assembly "as an accurate summary of attitudes and understandings within the denomination today and a helpful guide for further study and search to enable greater commonality of understanding and practice."

Encouraging congregations to study the role of women in the church was interpreted by many leaders and lay persons as opening ourselves to destructive forces, particularly the "women's lib" movement. No doubt this accounts in part for the reluctance to study this issue though it was recommended for study by General Assembly. Clearly, the purpose of the study was not intended to endorse the "women's lib" movement, but to provide a way of dealing constructively with a crucial and emotionally laden subject within the context of the church and Christian experience.

During the 1973-75 biennium, the Sunnyside congregation, of which Dennis Kuhns is pastor, was one of the few Mennonite congregations to study the issue. As the author's preface states, his treatment of this subject reflects his personal search and study along with that of his congregation over a period of several years.

I believe the author's discussion of this timely subject will help us to move beyond some of the prejudices and barriers which have obstructed our understanding and prevented us from appropriating fully the new order which Christ came to initiate and which He continues to make operative through the power of the Holy Spirit.

May God use this gift of the written word to enable us to "let the church be the church" in its truest sense!

Beulah Kauffman
Associate Secretary
Mennonite Board of Congregational Ministries
Elkhart, Indiana

February 17, 1978

1
WHAT IS THE CHURCH?

Since I believe one's understanding of the church is crucial to the topic under discussion, I would like to begin by outlining my understanding of the church. For this brief survey, I give credit to C. Norman Kraus from whose book, *The Community of the Spirit,* I have borrowed heavily. Kraus points out that for years we have been told that the Christian gospel or good news is about the events which fulfilled the promises God had made through the prophets to Israel. "The gospel actually happened! Jesus of Nazareth came as the promised Messiah and through His resurrection from the dead was 'designated Son of God with power by the Holy Spirit' (Romans 1:3, 4)."[1] But he goes on to note, "What has not been said with equal clarity and conviction is that the events of the first Christian Pentecost were a part of this incarnation drama."[2]

In his first chapter Kraus shows that Pentecost was

11

very much a part of the incarnation drama, not incidental to it. He says, "We conclude . . . that the gospel and salvation of which Jesus and His apostles spoke included the events of Pentecost. In these events the promise became a continuing reality. The mission which Jesus inaugurated in His earthly ministry was continued through the presence of His Holy Spirit in His new body."[3] "What really happened at Pentecost," Kraus points out later, "was the forming of the new community of the Spirit."[4] In this perspective, where Pentecost is seen as an integral part of the gospel, to be saved means "to participate in this new social reality created by the Spirit of Christ and offered to the world."[5] Or as Kraus says elsewhere, "Salvation means the restoration of a covenant relationship between God and man and man and his fellowman."[6]

Sin by contrast means "broken relationship. It is rejection of God's goodness and at the same time a refusal to love. It's most obvious manifestations are selfish competition, fearful struggle for survival, and prideful discrimination which destroy the possibility of personal fulfillment in a community of love."[7]

That the early church saw itself as a part of the promises of God given under the old covenant and a continuation of the ministry of Christ can be shown when we look at the New Testament. The concept of the church as a continuation of the ministry of Christ, empowered by His Spirit, is central to Paul's teaching that the church is the "body of Christ." The fact that the church is the fulfillment of God's promises can be seen in Peter's sermon on the day of Pentecost where he quotes the prophecy from Joel 2:28-32, and says that which the people in Jerusalem saw happening that day was the fulfillment of Joel's prophecy.

Wherever this community of faith (which I am calling the church) is experiencing God's saving, ruling presence, there the kingdom of God is manifest. "But even as we acknowledge its presence, we pray that it may come in its consummate fullness. . . . . The church is not the kingdom, yet proclaims the 'good news of the kingdom' and the 'keys of the kingdom' have been entrusted to it."[8] In this sense we can say each "congregation [is] . . . an outpost of God's kingdom ruled from heaven."[9] Each congregation, no matter how small or large, must evidence the signs of the kingdom of God demonstrating such qualities as love, joy, peace, and patience. This means breaking down the dividing walls of hostility that separate people from God and from each other (racism, sexism, greed, and the like).

It is clear from the Scriptures that this new life which the believers live as the church is not something they do on their own strength. For example, 2 Corinthians 5 ties the new life of the believers to the death and resurrection of Jesus Christ. Paul says that Christ's "purpose in dying for all was that men, while still in life, should cease to live for themselves, and should live for him who for their sake died and was raised to life" (v. 15, NEB). Having made this point, Paul continues, "With us therefore worldly standards have ceased to count in our estimate of any man; even if once they counted in our understanding of Christ, they do so now no longer. When anyone is united to Christ, there is a new world; the old order has gone, and a new order has already begun" (vv. 16-17, NEB).

This is a most profound statement. But it is one that has largely been ignored by contemporary Christianity.

In essence Paul is saying that to experience the new life of Jesus Christ is to experience a change in the way we look at others. The standards of our surrounding society no longer count in our estimation of anyone. Only Jesus Christ, His life, and love is the norm by which we live. In the words of Guy Hershberger, believers "share the spirit of the Suffering Servant"[10] in their relationships with all people.

This way of self-sacrificing love is the "supernatural order" through which believers promote and impliment the correction of wrong and injustice. It is "the way of love, of suffering, and of the cross which alone can restore sinful men to the way of loving obedience. [Their] . . . responsibility is that of calling sinful men to repentance, and of leading them to the way of the cross, bringing them into reconciliation with God and their fellowmen."[11]

This is my understanding of the church—a community of people redeemed out of every tribe, tongue, and nation to be God's people on earth now as well as in the age to come. This has profound implications for our discussion of the changing role of women in the church—implications that I hope to point out along the way.

2

WOMEN AND THE OLD TESTAMENT

A Summary View of Humanity at Creation

Much of the debate on the changing role of women in the church hinges on the relationship of man to woman and woman to man. From the Creation accounts and the account of the Fall, traditional Jewish and Christian teaching have postulated that relationship as one of woman's subjection to man in a heirarchy of authority.[12]

Interestingly, much of the traditional view is built on Genesis 2 and 3, with little discussion of Genesis 1:26,27. But as Dorothy Yoder Nyce has pointed out, "Each Creation account must be interpreted in relation to the other. Neither story dare be discarded or emphasized at the expense of the other."[13]

Genesis 1:26, 27 tells us that we (male and female) are: "(1) created to have dominion over the earth; (2) made to live in the relation of man and woman; (3) images and likenesses of the divine being."[14] It is important to note

15

that in the passage itself, and in Thielicke's summary, the creation of humanity as male and female was deliberate. There is nothing in these verses to indicate that the sexual difference between man and woman was a result of sin.[15] It was God's intention from the beginning that humanity would exist in His creation as male and female, with interdependence on each other and dependence on God. Indeed, as Paul Jewett observes, "The primal form of humanity is the fellowship of man and woman."[16] He goes so far as to claim that humanity's sexuality is very much a part of what it means to be created in the image of God. He says, " . . . the text of Genesis 1:27 makes no direct comment on Man in the image of God save to observe that he exists as male and female."[17]

The second biblical narrative of the creation of humanity is found in Genesis 2:7, 18, 21-25. In this account the male is created first, then the female is created from the rib of the male. Further, it is stated that the female is to be a "helper fit for him." Humanity created in God's image is not mentioned.

Traditional theological teaching has made much use of this passage. Since woman is created from man's rib and after the man, and she is created to be a "helper" for him, then man must be her "head" and she must be "subject" to him. Some past theologians went so far as to say this proved her inferiorty to the male.[18]

Such an interpretation of Genesis 2 is inconsistent with the affirmation of Genesis 1. In Genesis 1, we have "a picture of man and woman created for cooperative work in loving response to the will of the Creator in whose image they were made."[19] There is no implication of the inferiority of woman either ontologically (i.e., in her nature or being), or functionally. A study of the word "man" in Genesis 1:26, 27 reinforces this conviction. "Man" is used in the generic sense.[20] That is, "man" means mankind or humanity in general.

A study of the word "helper" in verse 18 of Genesis 2 may clear up our understanding of this passage. It has been pointed out that this same word, in Hebrew, is used elsewhere in the Old Testament in speaking of God as humanity's helper.[21] Moses used this same word in reference to God as he gave the reason for naming one of his sons Eliezer.[22] This word is used in the Psalms where God is seen as Israel's "help and shield" in time of trouble.[23] *Strong's Exhaustive Concordance of the Bible* indicates that the word translated as "help" or "helper" in these passages comes from the same Hebrew word meaning "to surround, i.e., to protect or aid."[24] The word clearly has a deeper meaning in Genesis 2 than we have traditionally ascribed to it. It describes a relationship of mutual interdependence, rather than the woman existing for the male's convenience, or as his underling.

Clemens summarizes the meaning of "helper" well: "Built into man's nature is his dependency upon God for a sustaining relationship that develops his personhood and gives it meaning and purpose. Over and over the Old Testament shows God being this kind of help to man. Likewise woman brings to man a human relationship through which he becomes a more complete person. No other living creature could provide such companionship for him; there had to be one who was like him and yet distinct from him."[25]

The rib, in Genesis 2, characterizes the closeness and yet the distinction between man and woman. The

17

woman is very much a part of the man, and can share with him in life's experiences. This, the other creatures of the earth could not do. The sequence of the account supports this view. When God said it was not good for the man to be alone, we are told that God then created every beast of the field, every bird of the air, and brought them to the man to see what he would call them. But no helper fit for the man was found. Then, it is said, God caused a sleep to come upon the man, and He took one of the man's ribs and formed the woman. Now there is someone like the man with whom he can share life's experiences on an intimate level, someone who can give him mutual support. She can share with him because she is like him. Yet she is distinct from him and can give him what he does not possess in himself. And, the reverse is true as well. This interpretation of Genesis 2 supports that of Genesis 1—that the primal form of humanity is the fellowship of man and woman.

The Image of God and Human Sexuality

We cannot study the Creation accounts and discuss the relationship between man and woman that they teach without reflecting on what it means to be created in the "image of God." Neither can we study them without reflecting upon what it means to be male and female, masculine or feminine.

The idea of the "image of God" has been discussed at great length by theologians.[26] Richard Mouw says that traditionally two human attributes have been "singled out as likely explanations for the meaning of the references to God's image."[27] Some refer to humanity's rational capacities (i.e., humanity's ability to think and reason). Others refer to humanity's spiritual dimension.

For example, Hershberger says, "Man in his original nature was like a mirror reflecting God's holiness and love in a relationship of responsive obedience."[28] Or, to take an example from one of the historic confessions of faith, God is said to have "created man, male and female, after his own image, in knowledge, righteousness, and holiness."[29]

This way of defining the "image of God" is not as popular today. "A common complaint is that such traditional interpretations impose an alien philosophical framework onto the biblical account."[30]

Recently the theological discussion has focused on the "social dimension of human nature," or the "office to which the human pair was assigned with respect to the rest of Creation."[31] Karl Barth defined the image of God in terms of human nature's social dimensions. He said, "Is it not astonishing that again and again expositions have ignored the definitive explanation given by the text itself. . . ? Could anything be more obvious than to conclude from this clear indication that the image and likeness of the being created by God signifies existence in confrontation, i.e., in this confrontation, in the juxtaposition and conjuction of man and man which is that of male and female. . . ?[32] Paul Jewett follows Barth in this understanding of the image of God in the quotation cited earlier and in the whole argument of his book.[33]

Mouw comments on the weakness of this argument, "It is not immediately clear that being 'male and female' is a way of resembling God; nor does this characteristic provide us with an unambiguous means for distinguishing humans from many animals who, from all appearance, participate in heterosexual relationships."[34] Further, this argument tends to elevate the male/female relationship to such a degree that it excludes other important human relationships.

The other contemporary definition of the "image of God" focuses on the "office" given to humanity at creation. Using the assignment given in Genesis 1:28 and stressing Psalm 8:4-8, this interpretation says that God's image has to do with having dominion over the earth, with representing God in His creation. However this interpretation "cannot be firmly established either."[35] What does it mean to have dominion?

All of this shows us that to understand what it means to be in God's image is not easy. As Mouw concludes, ". . . we ought not to ignore the possibility that 'image of God' refers to something more complex than any of the simple hypotheses we have mentioned."[36]

Reviewing all the attempts at definition, we become aware that "human beings were created for positive, social, cooperation with each other, in obedience to the will of the Creator. It is not just that human beings were created to be social, but that they were meant to be social in certain ways."[37]

If Mouw is correct, then each of us (male and female) best reflects the image of God when we are in relationship with another human being in a positive cooperative way. In borrowing from the more traditional definition, we can define that "positive cooperative" relationship as being one where the righteousness and love of God are manifest. The more we reflect that righteousness and love in our relationships the clearer we mirror God's image. To the degree we do not reflect these attributes God's image is distorted.

If this is true between persons of the same sex, then it is also true between persons of the opposite sex. "Men

20

and women were not meant to be two independent, self-subsistent individuals having no need of each other. Rather, they are made to be one dual being in a totality consisting of two distinct persons, one male and the other female . . . naturally oriented toward each other."[38] Hershberger makes a similar point, when in commenting on the functional difference between male and female he says, "The fact that there are functional differences . . . makes it all the more necessary that in all of life there be a close cooperation between man and woman; for if one of them must work alone, and the function of the other be omitted, life will be so much the poorer."[39] It is together, then, as they cooperate on many different levels of human relationship,[40] that men and women incorporate the "image of God." While this can perhaps be said to be true to a limited degree among all human beings, it is definitely to be expected among Christians whose encounters with each other are enriched by the Spirit of Him who is confessed to be the "image of the invisible God" (Colossians 1:15).

Having noted that there are functional differences between men and women, we must now consider the nature of masculinity and femininity. Are there concrete differences between men and women beyond the obvious biological ones?

The answer is as fleeting as an answer to what it means to be created in the "image of God." Perhaps there is a reason for this—since they are both so wrapped up with our understanding of ourselves, and we all remain (to some extent) a mystery to our own selves. At any given point in time we never fully understand who we are. All of life is a process of unraveling the mystery of our own identity.[41]

21

Sherwin Bailey says there are two reasons why "it is impossible to attempt any exact definition of manhood, or womanhood."[42] The first reason is that sexual knowledge is the kind which cannot easily be expressed, communicated, or formulated. "Otherwise, there would be no difficulty in detecting and correcting false conceptions of what is manly or womanly." The second reason is that our human relationships, through which we gain understanding of masculinity and femininity, vary so much depending on the persons and circumstances involved that definition is excluded.[43]

However, having said that, Bailey insists that any understanding of one's sexuality (masculinity or femininity) will be obtained only in relationship with another of the complementary sex. "Alone, or with another of one's own sex, one is not conscious of sex as a personal quality," he observes.[44] However, "to enter into sincere relations (of whatever kind) with a member of the complementary sex is to move into a new dimension of experience through encounter with another who is human, but in a radically different way from oneself—who is so like one, yet so very unlike. Now, and only now, does sex become meaningful as a personal quality."[45] He later adds, "The significance of [sexuality] . . . consists not in what I am in myself, but in what I am for another [of the complementary sex]."[46] Bailey is convinced that this is as far as we can go, and that "it is impossible to attempt any exact definition of manhood and womanhood."[47]

Apparently sexuality, like being in the image of God, refers to something more complex than any simple hypotheses we can formulate. The mystery of our own being prevents us from finding any easy answers. But the insight that Bailey brings shows the error of the kinds of artifical separation between men and women that have been perpetrated in every human society. To repeat Hershberger's statement, "The fact that there are differences . . . makes it all the more necessary that in all of life there be a close cooperation between men and women."[48] A little later he says, "It is obvious that a home without a mother will suffer through the absence of an essential functionary. It should be just as obvious, however, that a home without a father will suffer likewise. If this is true in the home it is equally true that the church, the school, and the community will suffer to the extent that either the male or female element of the population fails, for whatever reason, to function as it ought. God has created the human both a social and a sexual being. No one, therefore, can function as a normal human being except as a member of society. Neither can that society function as God intended that it should without the full and free cooperation of both its male and female constituents."[49]

The Fall and the Decline of the Role of Women

Genesis 3 tells of the fall of humanity into sin.[50] Sin resulted in separation from God (Genesis 3:8-10). The man and the woman hid themselves from God when He came into the garden to be with them. Instead of greeting God in glad expectation, the couple hid from Him in fear and shame.

Sin not only separated them from God, but it separated them from each other as well. Verse 7 says, "Then the eyes of both were opened, and they knew that they were naked; and they sewed fig leaves together and made themselves aprons." This is a startling statement in light of the last verse in chapter 2, "the man and his wife were both naked, and were not ashamed." Vernard Eller, commenting on the significance of the change between Genesis 2 and 3, says, ". . . the point of our first parents' nakedness is that there is nothing between them—not so much as a blush of shame. No barriers, no secrets, no regrets, no facades, no intimidations, no status distinctions, no suspicion. The relationship is that of frankness, honesty, trust, openness, 'here-I-amness,' nakedness. 'Shame'—which is the condign and involuntary admission that one is in the wrong—is the worst possible thing that could come between, for it is itself the sign of other deep and serious barriers."[51] Before they sinned there was mutual trust; afterward there was fear, suspicion, shame—the need to protect themselves. Thus they covered themselves.

The "curse" portions of this chapter have been used to reinforce the traditional pattern of man/woman relationships. Subjection is imposed on woman because she was the first to sin. This is seen as evidence of her moral and spiritual weakness. So God said the man "shall rule over you."[52] The weakness in this argument, however, is the failure to consider the forgiveness of God and the victory of Jesus Christ. The picture of God in the Bible is that of unreserved forgiveness at repentance.[53] Also, the Bible says that Jesus Christ destroyed sin and its effects.

Rather than viewing these pronouncements as prescribing for all time the present roles of men and women as the will of God, they can be viewed as describing the outcome of humanity's sin. Dorothy Yoder Nyce says, "The judgment of Genesis three is the Creator's acknowledgement of the fallen world."[54] Or, as Robert

Hartzler puts it, "The sin list is descriptive and not prescriptive. It says this is what happens, it does not say this is the way it always has to be."[55]

This interpretation can be tested by going to the passage itself. God neither fully accepts nor denies the excuse each character in the account offers for their disobedience. Each is responsible for their own sin and they are party to the sin of the other. As we look at what God says to each character, it is interesting to note that the serpent and the ground are "cursed," while neither the man nor the woman are "cursed." Verses 14 and 17, speaking to the serpent and refering to the earth, are the only two statements that could be understood as direct commands prescribing the will of God.

Turning to the pronouncements to the man and the woman, there is a difference. God's words to the woman are that in spite of the pain of childbirth, she shall desire her husband. The phrase "he shall rule over you" appears more as a statement of fact describing her condition rather than a commmand. Each translation I consulted could be interpreted this way.[56] Significantly *The Jerusalem Bible* translates the last part of verse 16, "Your yearning shall be for your husband, yet he will lord it over you." Further, in light of the traditional interpretation of the pronouncement to the woman as prescribing God's will for all time, it is interesting to see in God's pronouncement to the man that He doesn't even mention the relationship between the man and woman. The total statement to the man is given over to the changed relationship between the man and the earth. Bread will now be gotten only by the "sweat of your face."

In effect then, "work, for both man and woman,

25

expresses the division of fallen mankind with each other and with the cursed nature. Man is now associated with the task of conquering nature, woman with the burdens involved in reproduction. . . . Mary Daly suggests that 'isolated in fixed sex roles, they are no longer partners in all things.' But there is no indication that this must continue forever. Rigid sex roles are a result of sin, not characteristics of nature.''[57]

A possible view of the development of rigid sex roles with the advent of the Fall is simply that they developed along biological lines. The male not having to carry the child in his body during gestation was free to do the more strenuous work necessary for survival—tilling the soil, hunting, and the like. By necessity the male became aggressive. The ground was "cursed" and only by sweat and toil would it bring forth food. Also, there were other aggressive males to compete with for food and water. Such traits as brute strength, and power over others, became the marks of true manhood which were admired.

The woman, however, had to bear the child in her body. She had to protect herself if the child was to survive. Her role developed around the home, focusing on the domestic chores and care of the young. By necessity the qualities of intuitivness, compassion, and gentleness developed as her attention was given to the care of the household. Ideal womanliness became more and more defined as a passive, meek, quiet, unassertive nature, always in the shadow of the male who was the provider.

The final stage of this development was inevitable. Such narrowly defined roles only increased the separation between the male and the female that happened at the Fall. The further apart they grew, the less they understood each other. Finally, woman was believed at best to be inferior to man and at the worst feared as evil.[58] Clemens summarizes this well, "In most human cultures, woman is considered a lower human being than the male, less wise, less intelligent than he, and lacking in many of his capabilities and abilities. It is evident that when woman must be the cricket on the hearth caring for the young while the man is the eagle on the wing broadening his experiences and increasing his observations, her limited experiences make her appear less highly endowed than man."[59]

Woman in the Old Testament

We have observed that domination and rigid sex roles are characteristics of the Fall. This can be seen in every human civilization from the beginning of recorded history to the present. It can be seen in the life of Israel.

It is clear that the world of the Old Testament was a "man's world." During that time women were considered little more than property. It should not surprise us that this is reflected in Jewish life and culture as well. Paul Jewett gives an excellent overview of the place of women in Jewish society during the centuries covered by the Old Testament. Space will allow only a brief summary.[60] A daughter remained under the authority of her father till she came under the authority of the man to whom she was given in marriage (note Saul's giving Michal to David). It was the custom of the groom to pay for the bride with money, animals, and even work (such as Jacob working for Rachel). When married, if the wife did not present her husband with a son, such reproach was cast upon her that she would sometimes have recourse to doubtful expedients (such as Sarah giving Hagar to Abraham; Rachel giving Bilhah to Jacob). If the husband died and had no son, his brother was to take the wife as his own to raise up descendants to the deceased. Though the man could refuse such a marriage, the woman could not.

We could go on listing other examples and touch on the purification rites and their effect on the place of women in Jewish society and life. But these only reinforce the picture already developing in the above examples. The net result was that women came to be considered inferior to men and "there emerged in Judaism an overt contempt for the female sex."[61] It is interesting to note that in the early Hebrew society of the Patriarchs, women mixed more freely with men than at later times. For example, Rebekah and the maidens came outside the city for water and talked with Abraham's servant. And later Ruth and her contemporaries gleaned in the fields of Boaz.[62] It would appear that settlement and standardization of Jewish society resulted in the greater restriction of women in Jewish life that characterized the time of Jesus.

These restrictions grew out of a distorted understanding of the law given to Israel. The religion was largely male oriented.[63] God was identified as masculine with an exclusive male priesthood. It may be that this was a deliberate attempt to counteract the licentiousness of the fertility cults of the surrounding pagan societies[64] whose gods displayed much of the same immoral behavior as their worshipers. But, rather than reinforcing the Genesis assertion that God is above and beyond sexual distinction, this orientation was distorted into male domination and exclusiveness. The rite of circumcision, seen as a distinctive mark of the covenant, provided another source of male exclusiveness. These elements of the Jewish religion, in time, provided the seedbed for some of the thought and practice that had developed by the time of Jesus.

Before we judge the Old Testament teachings too harshly or regard the Old Testament laws as sexist, we need to see them over against the surrounding cultures. There are indeed similarities. But we believe that God gave the law to Israel to be His instruments of revelation to the world. Similarities between the Jewish law and culture of the Old Testament and the practices of surrounding pagan cultures existed because God gave His law in the midst of a world that was male oriented to the extreme. The dissimilarity can be seen in the high honor accorded women despite the male orientation and later distortions. The law's intention was to protect women in the same way it sought to protect the slave and the stranger. The laws that we may react to as "sexist" in reality insured women a place and kept them from exploitation. That these laws were at times distorted and turned into male exclusivism is a matter of human weakness and not deliberate intent.[65] Distortion in the practice of the law is the focus of the prophets warnings.

Dispite the male orientation (and later distortions), it is striking to see the role women did play in Jewish history and religion. For example Hannah offered prayers and sacrifices for herself. Beyond this is leadership that certain women offered at various times in Old Testament history. Miriam, the sister of Moses and Aaron, is mentioned as a prophetess (Exodus 15:20). Later the prophet Micah in speaking to Israel says that Miriam was one whom God sent before them along with Moses and Aaron (Micah 6:4). King Josiah sent to a woman, Huldah, who was a prophetess, for a word from the

Lord (2 Kings 22). Her advice about needed reforms was heeded.

I mention Miriam and Huldah for a reason. It is often said that God will only call women to various types of leadership service if no able men are on the scene. But Miriam and Huldah served when there were competent men available in Israel: Miriam with Moses and Aaron, Huldah during the time of Jeremiah. It is not true that God only calls women when men are not or will not make themselves available.

Other women who served in Israel are: Deborah (Judges 4), who functioned as prophet, judge, and warrior; Esther, who by her dedication saved her people from destruction; Ruth, who is remembered by her dedication and love to her mother-in-law and her name on a book of the Bible just as in Esther's case.[66]

These are only the most obvious illustrations of women who served Israel under God. Dorothy Yoder Nyce reports that between Deuteronomy and 2 Kings there are 175 references to women serving in various capacities. In the same section, she finds twenty references to men and women serving in equal capacity.[67]

One Old Testament passage often used to enforce the place of women in their culturally defined role is Proverbs 31:10-31. This passage is often quoted as the ideal picture of the role of woman as wife and mother. However, Proverbs 31 gives a much broader definition of that role than is implied in much of the traditional teaching taken from it. She is pictured as a wise manager of the household (vv. 11-15, 21, 22, 27); a wise merchant and farm manager (vv. 16-19, 24); and as charitable (v. 20). Rather than being overly dependent, she is pictured as self-confident and assured (v. 25); a good teacher (v.

26); and one in whom her husband and children can place confidence and whom they praise (vv. 28, 29). Obviously this does not describe as free a lifestyle as women know today. But I am impressed with the breadth of freedom that the poem describes in light of the growing restrictions that developed later in Judaism (i.e., restriction to the house, and limited contact with men).[68]

3

WOMEN AND THE NEW TESTAMENT

Jesus and Women

When we turn to the New Testament, and specifically to the Gospels, we discover that Jesus did not say anything that sharply contrasted with the custom of His day regarding the question of woman's place in society.[69] "It is not so much in what He said as how He related to women that Jesus was a revolutionary."[70] As Clemens says, "Jesus' personal attitude toward womankind was not summarized by Him in any formal statement. He rather taught His doctrine of women in a much more forceful manner than mere words. In a day when the religious leaders thought it disreputable to so much as greet a woman in public—even if this was a wife or daughter or sister—Jesus openly conversed with women wherever He encountered them."[71]

In the Gospels we see evidence that Jesus appreciated the spiritual and intellectual capabilities of women.

Note two examples.[72] In John 4, Jesus talked with the woman of Samaria openly despite the prevailing prejudice against Samaritans and the attitudes that men ought not to talk openly with women. Note the depth of insight she had into the matters discussed (vv. 20, 25). Note too that Jesus declares Himself openly to her, something He did not often do with men (v. 26). Nor does Jesus challenge her witness.

The second example is Jesus' encounter with Mary and Martha in Luke 10:38-42. Upon Jesus' arrival in their home, Mary sat down with Jesus to discuss matters pertaining to the kingdom. Martha, however, was involved with "much serving" (v. 40). When Martha complained to Jesus about Mary's behavior, He rebuked Martha, saying Mary had chosen the better part. He thereby indicated where the priorities lay with Him.

Not only did Jesus appreciate the intellectual and spiritual capabilities of women, but He freely accepted services from them and "intimate"[73] contact with them. For example, Luke 8:2, 3 records that a number of women "provided for" Jesus and His disciples from their means. Luke 7:36-50[74] tells of a woman who anointed Jesus feet. Luke gives no name, but implies a woman of ill repute. Jesus cut across custom (see v. 39) and accepted her ministrations.

A final example of Jesus accepting contact with women is found in Luke 8:42b-48. Luke tells of a woman with a "flow of blood." She had been afflicted with this problem for twelve years. In light of the social taboo that had grown up around the law concerning female uncleanness (Leviticus 15:19-30) this problem placed a great hardship on the woman.[75] The woman finally sought out Jesus and in open public, despite social taboo and the danger of public censure, touched Jesus' garments. This act, by strict interpretation of the law, made Jesus ceremonially unclean and all who would come in contact with him. Yet Jesus did not rebuke her. Rather he commended her faith. Then, without feeling any need to go and seek cleansing according to the tradition, Jesus proceeded immediately to Jarius' house and raised his daughter from the dead.

Jesus did not discriminate socially, nor was gender a barrier in His spiritual teaching. He simply taught people, recognized women as persons of full worth, and allowed them contact with Him and the benefit of His thinking. Women were present on the occasion of feeding the 5,000 (Matthew 14:21) and He used parables about women to illustrate theological truths. He did so without any apparent qualm that God, whom He called "Father," might be identified as feminine. Note, for example, Luke 15:8 ff, the parable of the woman and the lost coin. In this parable, the woman looking for the lost coin represents God.[76]

Women in the Early Church

We turn now to the early church. The formation of the church took place on the day of Pentecost when the Holy Spirit came upon 120 believers in an upper room in Jerusalem. Acts records that women were present in the room and that the Holy Spirit came upon the whole group. The women shared equally in the experience. And, when Peter later quotes Joel's prophecy, he quotes it all including the part, " . . . and your daughters shall prophesy, . . . and on my menservants and my maidservants in those days I will pour out my Spirit; and they shall prophesy" (Joel 2:28b; Acts 2:17, 18).

What is significant in this prophecy is not that God said He would send His Spirit. He had been doing that in some degree all through the history of His people. Nor is it particularly notable that women are included. As we have seen, God at various times raised up women to do His work. The important change prophesied in Joel is that God anticipated a general outpouring of His Spirit rather than an outpouring upon a select few for a specific period of time as under the old covenant. "Upon all flesh" in the context of Joel's prophecy means an outpouring upon all God's people for all time. Within the church the broken relationships caused by sin are restored.

Peter, along with the early church, recognized this as being fulfilled in their midst, and women as being equally involved in that blessing! Indeed "all flesh" takes on a still broader meaning as Peter and the church realize the blessing is extended to believing Gentiles as well. Now the "chosen people of God" are not the Jews by physical birth, but Jews and Gentiles who have experienced spiritual rebirth. The church is, then, the practical expression of Paul's meaning when he says Christ broke "down the dividing wall of hostility . . . that he might create in himself one new man" (Ephesians 2:14 ff).

The effect can be seen immediately. Women, who under Judaism played only a minor role in worship, now assumed a more prominent role in the church. They were present at the prayer meetings and active in works of charity. Besides aiding the apostles, they often opened their homes as places of worship.

The story of Lydia (Acts 16) is of particular interest in this light. Women were not considered as members of the congregation of Jewish synagogues. "In order for a congregation to exist there had to be at least ten men; nine men plus all the women of Israel would not be sufficient."[77] Over against this attitude was the formation of the church at Philippi in Lydia's house. Paul went out to the river which he accepted as a place of prayer. There he preached to a group of women. These women became the nucleus of the Philippian church.

In Acts we discover Christian women were prophetesses (Philip's daughters in Acts 21:9). Some were teachers, such as Priscilla who along with Aquila expounded the word more perfectly to Apollos (Acts 18:26). Unusual for that time is the way Paul mentions Priscilla's name before her husband's in some of his letters. "Scholars of early church history suggest that perhaps she had edited Paul's letters before they were sent out to the churches. It has been established that she was with Paul when his letters of Philippians, Philemon, and Colossians are believed to have been sent out from Rome in revised form. Therefore, Priscilla is considered as a probable editor of these letters."[78] Some scholars have nominated her as the author of the letter to the Hebrews.[79]

Paul's letters give evidence to the prominent role women played in the early church. Nine of the twenty-six people Paul mentions by name in Romans 16 are women. A woman, Phoebe, heads the list. She is called a *Diakonos,* translated "deaconess" in the RSV and "servant" in the KJV. While these translations are possible, reflecting an area of meaning in the word, they hide the fact that Paul uses this same word to refer to himself and others of the apostles in which case the word is translated as minister or deacon.

Smith's *Greek-English Concordance* shows that *DIAKONOS* appears a total of thirty times in the New Testament. In the KJV it is translated twenty times as "minister," its meaning ranging from aid rendered to another and to designate one who gives such aid, to a name used to designate the apostles themselves. Seven times in the KJV *Diakonos* is translated as "servant" and three times as "deacon."[80] The weight of evidence indicates that Phoebe was more than someone who "served at the tables." She was evidently "in the service of the church along with the men."[81] At this point some warn that "to see in Phoebe evidence for an established order of deaconess or for female officals in the church is more than the evidence warrants."[82] The point is well made. However, let us be careful not to down play Phoebe's significance so much that we miss the dramatic role she and other women apparently had in the early church when viewed against the background of their time.

Paul mentions Euodia and Syntyche in Philippians 4. The words he uses in referring to these women in verse 3 as having "labored side by side with me" means "participation in the proclamation of the gospel."[83]

"Never in the history of the Christian Church has woman ever taken such a prominent part in [the proclamation of the gospel] . . . as in the first centuries of the Christian era."[84] However, as the church spread and grew, and as standardization of church structure was accomplished, a gradual decline of women's responsibilities in it occured. "The church fathers placed more and more prohibitions on women's participation in church life. The numerous restrictions imposed upon them in the pronouncements of the various councils point out the many ways in which women had been functioning prior to that time. They also indicate why one pagan writer's observation had been: 'what women there are among the Christians.' "[85] By the time of Constantine, the church organization had become all male, and women sought new avenues for expressing their Christian commitment. They founded women's cloisters, hospices for pilgrims, schools, and hospitals.[86]

With the advent of the Reformation, women began to find a more active place again. Here I speak from my own denominational history as a Mennonite. Among the Anabaptists, one out of every three martyrs to die for the faith was a woman. "Women appear on every page of *Martyrs Mirror* from page 420 on."[87] (*Martyrs Mirror* contains more than 1100 pages!) Further evidence of the prominent role women played can be found in the sketches of ten women written by Esther K. Augsburger for the Women's Missionary and Service Commission *Devotional Guide for 1975-1976.*[88] And this is only scratching the surface. We have yet to learn what historians will find when they explore the role of women in the Anabaptist and other free church movements.

More recent in Mennonite history is the story of Ann Jemima Allenbach. She was ordained to the preaching ministry in Philadelphia by the Eastern District churches of the General Conference Mennonite Church on January 15, 1911. Her work was largely in New York City and reflected great insight and compassion.[89]

Lest we idealize the role of women, we should note that the attitude of Anabaptist leaders was similar to that of the general culture of that time.[90] And in some extreme groups, such as the Muensterites, there is evidence of oppression of women. However, the Ana-

38

baptist and other free church movements reflect a return to a more prominent role for women in the local congregations than was possible in state churches.

The Teaching of Paul and Peter

When we turn to the Epistles, we come to those passages which form the watershed for much of the debate surrounding the changing role of women in the church. In 1 Corinthians 11:2-16, Paul discusses the use of the veil, saying the husband is "head of the wife." And in 1 Corinthians 14:33b-36 Paul instructs women to be silent in the church. This passage is paralled in 1 Timothy 2:11 ff. The other passages are Ephesians 5:21 ff., paralleled in Colossians 3:18 ff., where wives are told to be "subject" to their husbands. Peter makes a smiliar statement in 1 Peter 3:1 ff.

Several attitudes can be taken concerning these passages. First, we could ignore them, claiming that Paul, or Peter, were at a lower level of understanding here than in Galatians 3:28 where Paul says in Christ there is neither male nor female. Jewett makes such an argument, saying that in the other passages Paul's thinking is still clouded by his rabbinic training.[91]

Another way of handling these passages is not to attribute them to Paul at all. Some scholars hold that Ephesians, Colossians, and the Pastoral Epistles are pseudepigraphal writings and cannot be used to indicate Paul's views.[92] Thus these passages can be ignored as reflecting later prejudice in a more highly structured church than existed in Paul's day. Some scholars accept as valid the theory that 1 Corinthians 14:33b-36 is a post-Pauline gloss added to the letter at a later time, and that it does not reflect Paul's true thinking.

39

Jewett notes that scholars give 1 Corinthians 14:33b-36 a "B" rating for authenticity.[93] However, it is still included in the texts of the Greek New Testaments,[94] and therefore is included in all versions of our English Bibles. We should point out that while a "B" rating indicates "some degree of doubt," on a scale from "A" to "D" the rating is not all that low.

The problem with these various attempts to ignore these passages, or to play the Paul you like against the Paul you don't like, is that the evidence is not all that conclusive. There are learned scholars on both sides of the issues involved. At this point in time, to draw the conclusions described in the two preceding paragraphs is far too radical. What criteria do we use to measure cultural expression and say this or that passage is not pertinent to our time? Or by what criteria do we say Paul was at a lower level of understanding here than elsewhere? In the end the criteria involved in the conclusions described, and in similar arguments is one's own subjective judgment. A question posed by John Howard Yoder indicates the weakness of such arguments: "How can there be any corrective challenge to our self-sufficiency, any continuity in the Christian community—to say nothing of any judging and redeeming word of God—if the present insight of the bearer is to be sovereign judge of any new communication he will accept?"[95]

The second method of approach in handling these passages involves the idea of an "order of Creation," and teaches that woman is subject to man based on a hierarchy of authority seen as laid down in Genesis 2 and 3 and 1 Corinthians 11. This approach says Paul is building on this order. This is the position reflected in

40

much of the popular Christian writing of our day on the subject of marriage and the family, [96] and in most of the theological works of the past and present. [97]

The problem with this position is that while it claims to be the biblical position, taking the Bible literally, it ignores the other biblical evidence. Do we forget the Gospels and Acts? Do we convienently ignore the rest of Paul's or Peter's letters, overlooking the implications of their understanding of the impact of the cross and the nature of the church? To do so is again to play the Paul you like against the Paul you don't like as some on the other side of this issue do. And we have no more certain word from God than before.

A further argument of the "order of Creation" view says that woman ought to be subject to man because it is "natural." Some use this line of thought in opposing the admission of women to certain leadership positions in the church. [98]

The assumption in this argument is that the basic roles of women and men have continued unchanged from Creation to the present. This argument fails to take into account that what may seem "natural" now, after the Fall, may not have been "natural" before the Fall. The argument does not allow for the effect of sin on human civilization and its structures. Considerable recent literature discusses this point. [99] To appeal to the nature of things as they are is to appeal to the nature of things in the fallen state, not as God originally created them. [100]

In light of the confession of historic Christian faith that humanity is born in sin, it is startling to see the bland acceptance of things as they are as criteria for Christian living—particularly acceptance of the structures of society. Historically, Christians have shown more optimism toward the "natural order" of things than toward the good of an individual. In Western Christendom particularly, discernment in accepting social convention has been lacking. We need to be aware that the structure of things as they are may be in fact quite contrary to God's will despite what may seem right. The weakness of trusting in "what seems natural" or "what feels right" is the same weakness inherent in "letting your conscience be your guide." Our feelings about what seems natural, as well as our consciences may be (and I believe are) conditioned by sin as it is individually and corporately expressed.

How Should We Live?

The key to interpreting the passages by Paul and Peter is to stay by the context where they are found. All of these passages are found in sections of the letters where the writers deal with the moral and ethical behavior of the Christians. Note, for example, in Ephesians that Paul moves from a discussion of the unity of the believers in Christ (4:1-10) to an appeal for them to "no longer live as the Gentiles do" (4:17-32) but to be "imitators of God as dear children . . . walking in love as Christ loved us" (5:1-20). It is in this context that Paul tells the Ephesian Christians to "be subject to one another out of reverence for Christ" (v. 21)[101] and then moves to his instructions for the households (vv. 22 ff.). The instructions to the households are specific applications of what it means to be Christian. They apply to one's family life what it means to be subject to one another out of reverence for Christ, walking in love as Christ loved us, to be imitators of God as dear children.

42

In Colossians we find a similar train of thought developing. Paul has just warned the believers to beware of teaching that is not "according to Christ" in whom they have come to fullness of life (2:8-15). The following section (vv. 16 ff.) is an explanation of verse 6, where he said, "As therefore you received Christ Jesus the Lord, so live in him." Having laid the foundation that Christ is the Source and Example of life for the Christian, Paul calls them to "put to death what is earthly . . . and to put on . . . compassion, kindness," and the like. It is in this context that Paul moves on to his instructions to the households in the Colossian church (3:18—4:1). Again he is making a specific application of what he has just said.

In 1 Corinthians 11:2-16 and 14:33b-36, the admonitions on the veiling and silence are part of the instructions Paul is giving about worship. Note how he builds on the idea of Christians being one in the body of Christ (10:31 ff.), finally calling them to be "imitators of me as I am of Christ" (11:1). From this appeal he moves into instructions concerning the veiling and communion. In chapter 14, the admonition for women to be silent is part of Paul's call for orderliness in worship which is applied to prophets and those speaking in tongues. We shall look more closely at these passages and 1 Timothy 2:11 ff. in the following pages.

Looking at 1 Peter 3:1-7, we notice that Peter's instructions to wives and husbands is a natural development of his appeal that Christians "abstain from the passions of the flesh that wage war against your soul" (2:11) and of his appeal to maintain good conduct among the Gentiles. Further, these instructions to the households are all part of Peter's understanding of the church as a "chosen race, a royal priesthood . . . God's own people, that you may declare the wonderful deeds of Him who called you out of darkness into his marvelous light" (2:9).

This overview of the Pauline and Petrine passages shows us that their understanding of Christ and His work, plus their understanding of the church as the "body of Christ," is the very backbone of their teaching to the households. With this understanding, we can now go back and discover Paul and Peter's intention in these passages.

It is the Christian's commitment to follow Christ in the way of self-giving love that Paul and Peter have in view. Christ's self-giving love forms the basis for the call to subjection and is the example of headship. Christian slaves are called upon to live out this kind of life in the situation where they find themselves (Ephesians 6:5 ff., Colossians 3:22 ff., 1 Peter 2:18 ff). Note how Peter ties his instructions to wives directly to his instructions to the slaves by use of the word "likewise" (3:1). Christians wives are to be a subject to their husbands "as to the Lord" (Ephesians 5:22b). This phrase probably carries the same meaning as Colossians 3:18 where Paul says, "As is fitting in the Lord."[102] In both cases the appeal to wives focuses on their decision to be disciples of Jesus Christ.

In the same way, Christian husbands are called upon to love their wives "as Christ loved the church and gave himself up for her" (Ephesians 5:25). Through His suffering, Christ cleansed the church and thus presents it to Himself without spot or wrinkle. In Colossians 3:19 the instruction to husbands does not contain a reference to Christ's self-sacrificing love. However in the context of the letter and specifically of the preceeding paragraph (vv. 12-17) the point could not be missed.

We will better understand Paul's appeal if we go back to the Gospels and look at Jesus' attitude and teaching about authority and power in His kingdom. At the last supper, according to Luke 22:24 ff.,[103] the disciples were arguing about positions of power and authority in the kingdom. Jesus reminds them that while the Gentiles have kings who exercise authority over them and who are called "benefactors," it will not be so among His followers. In His kingdom, among those who follow Him, the greatest will be as the youngest, and the leader (head?) will be as one who serves. Jesus makes His point by reminding them that He is among them as "one who serves." John's Gospel (chapter 13) adds to this scene by telling us how Jesus washed the disciples feet. John includes Jesus' own interpretation of his action:

> You call me Teacher and Lord; and you are right, for so I am. If I then, your Lord and Teacher, have washed your feet, you also ought to wash one another's feet. For I have given you an example, that you also should do as I have done to you. John 13:13-15.

Subjection and headship in Christ's kingdom have to do with serving others in self-sacrificing love. Paul makes his appeal for this kind of lifestyle among the believers at Philippi in the beautiful hymn recorded in Philippians 2:5-11. A look at this hymn will show us how Jesus' teachings in the Gospels on authority and power relate to Paul's and Peter's teachings on subjection and headship.

In Philippians 2, Paul tells us that Jesus did not seek to use His favored position as Son of God to "grasp" at

45

equality with God. Rather He chose to do the will of God. That is, He chose to become a man, but more than that to become as a slave, and then to die. Therefore, God raised Him from the dead and gave Him the position that was rightfully His from His preincarnate state. But that position is now granted because of His willingness to lay it aside and take the form of the Suffering Servant and die in obedience to God's will. By raising Him from the dead, by giving Him a "name which is above every name," God has established for all time and eternity the Suffering Servant model of life for all who would be known as children of God. The opening chapters of Ephesians and Colossians, devoted to Christ's work and his preeminence, further reinforce this lifestyle for all believers.

This Suffering Servant lifestyle means that the Christian's stance toward power and authority in this world is nonresistance, and toward culture it is nonconformity.[104] Therefore, Christian wives, slaves,[105] children, all who were not (and still are not in some cases) in positions of power by reason of society's conventions, are called upon to be nonresistant in their relationships to those in power. That is, they are called upon to be "subject" to them—not as an "order of creation," but for the Lord's sake living as free people, yet without using their freedom as a pretext for evil; but living as servants of God (1 Peter 2:13, 16).

For those Christians who are socially in positions of power and authority, the Suffering Servant lifestyle of Jesus calls them not to conform to the surrounding culture's definitions of their place and status. Rather, they are to follow Christ's example of lordship, being as "one who serves." As the Book of Philemon makes clear, the net result of this kind of living in the church, where two or three are gathered in the name of Christ, is that such social roles as master/slave, subjection of wife (or women)/headship of husband (or men), are destroyed. Even the relationship between parents and children is changed. In the church, there are only "brothers and sisters" in Christ. The subjection they live is not based on some social role, justified by some order of creation, but on mutual subjection to one another in reverence for Christ.

For those who would protest that this approach is too slow in bringing needed change in our society, I would point out that there is nothing here to prevent the church from speaking out against injustice in our culture. Indeed by existing as a community of love, peace, and justice in the midst of an unjust and wanton society, the church (in fact each congregation) is doing that very thing. And the Great Commission to go into all the world and preach the gospel presupposes it as well. Further, as Yoder, speaking of modern criticism of Paul's teaching on slavery says, "Modern judges of New Testament ethics generally do not bother to suggest what Paul in his situation should have done differently. What should an Emancipation Proclamation have looked like then? Did Lincoln's way really work? Nor do they generally note that the 'established' forms of 'Christendom' which legalized slavery were not obeying the ethics of either Jesus or Paul as we find them in this study. Nor do they generally bother to test whether some then available option (Islam?) would have had over the centuries a more liberating effect. . . ."[106] The same argument can be applied to modern criticism of Paul's teaching to women. Just what should an "Equal

Rights Amendment" of that time have looked like? In the end Christians should realize that the real impact of the church on society will not be by legislation, but by being the embodiment of Christ in our communities. As the embodiment of Christ, each congregation is the salt of the earth and the light of the world. The congregation that is not the salt of the earth and the light of the world is accommodating to the world, selling its birthright, and functioning simply as another institution in society.[107]

Yes, But Paul Still Says . . .

Having come this far, we have yet to deal with 1 Corinthians 11:3 (and a similar statement in Ephesians 5:23) and 1 Timothy 2:12 ff. (and a similar statement in 1 Corinthians 14:33 ff.). These statements form the touchstones for the teaching of an "order of creation," and thus as restrictions forbidding women to serve in certain offices of the church.

It is my own conviction that these passages say nothing more than what we have already observed. Paul is calling upon Christian women and men to use the conventional social roles, imposed by their culture, to live out the gospel. As Yoder says, "Since in the resurrection and in Pentecost the kingdom which was imminent has now in part come into our history, the church can now live out, within the structure of society, the newness of the life of the kingdom. The early church . . . transformed the concept of living within a role by finding how in each role the servanthood of Christ, the voluntary subordination of one who knows that another regime is normative, could be made concrete."[108]

Paul's argument for the continued use of the veiling in

1 Corinthians 11 illustrates this statement. Note verse 3.[109] If Paul is here speaking to husbands and wives specifically, and not to men and women in general (as implied in the KJV and other translations), then this verse is similar to that in Ephesians 5:23, and is a reminder for the Christian wife to give due respect to her husband. Thus following the example of Christ who voluntarily subjected Himself to God as His head, the wife is transforming her role, imposed by her culture, into an avenue of Christian servanthood. While Paul here is speaking to wives of their Christian duty, it is clear in other passages of Scripture that such respect for others is expected of all Christians—married or single, young or old, rich or poor.[110]

For the Christian wives at Corinth, part of what having respect for their husbands meant was not bringing dishonor to their husbands by disgarding the veil while participating in the worship service. "In that culture the veil symbolized the marriage relationship. If the wife appeared in public unveiled, it was considered a disgrace to the husband; it was as if she were dishonoring the marriage relationship. Paul therefore asks the Christian wives not to give the impression of renouncing the marriage relationship by violating their custom of public veiling."[111]

To strengthen his argument, Paul turns to the Creation account (vv. 8, 9). He reminds the wives that woman had her beginning from man (v. 8), and therefore she stands in relation to man as nothing else does in all creation.[112] This is the apparent meaning of the phrase, "But the woman is the glory of man." By appealing to Creation, Paul reminds Christian wives of the Creator's divine intention that woman was created to

49

live in mutual interdependence with man. She was not created to be an independent, self-subsistent being with no need of another anymore than man was. This reinforces the apostle's call to servanthood in marriage. And we can see how much the Christian life of servanthood, as lived by Christ, is a mirror of God's original intention for humanity.

Lest there be any misunderstanding of Paul's appeal for continued use of the veil at Corinth and an undue inferior status be imposed on women, verse 11 is a reminder of the true relationship that exists within the church (note the phrase "in the Lord"). There is a true interdependence within the people of God, the kind of interdependence God intended from the beginning. Paul illustrates this elsewhere with his analogy of the church as a "body."[113] And here he shows the same is true in the home. Lest the husband vaunt himself at the expense of the wife, Paul reminds the husband that man is now born of woman (v. 12). In the last verses of this section, Paul appeals to accepted propriety and the practice in other congregations to further strengthen his argument for use of the veiling.[114]

In 1 Corinthians 14 and 1 Timothy 2, we come to those passages often used to impose silence on women in the church. These verses are variously interpreted from a very severe restriction on a woman's participation in the life of the congregation (not being permitted to pray, read Scripture, or even take part in business meetings) to simply a restriction in the office that can be held by a woman. Such wide divergence should give everyone a sense of caution as we come to these passages.

At first glance these passages appear to contradict other statements by the apostle.[115] Clemens gives a brief summary of the attempts to reconcile the seeming contradictory statements.[116] For example, the Corinthian passage (chapter 14) may refer to an open meeting where unbelievers were present who might have misunderstood the freedom of the Christian wives in worship. The passage in chapter 11:5 was spoken with the closed meeting in mind, for example, a love feast where only believers were present. Further possible explanations refer to the church at Corinth meeting in the local Jewish synagogue and that the Jews were critical of the lack of respect the women had for synagogue law. Thus Paul asks them to abide by the rules. Of the Timothy passage, some authorities believe this was addressed to illiterate, repressed women recently emerged from heathendom, thus unfit to teach, or that this prohibition is synonymous with not usurping authority.

As stated earlier,[117] the key to interpreting these passages is to stay by the context in which they are found. The admonition for women to be silent in 1 Corinthians 14 is part of Paul's appeal for orderliness in worship. Dorothy Yoder Nyce says, "With women and prophets, orderliness in worship is still to be maintained, in spite of the new freedom found in Christ. The writer here suggests that married women pattern current Jewish law in order not to be offensive, that prophets and those speaking in tongues also avoid confusion. Today, there is still good reason for orderly, corporate worship and respect for the regulations or patterns of the non-Christian community in whose presence worship takes place. But this does not sanction that either prophets or women be excluded from giving responsible expression to the message of God's kingdom. Paul elsewhere, earlier in chapter 14 (vv 1 ff.) and in chapter

51

11 (v. 5), accepts without question the fact of women prophesying and praying in public, serving as worship leaders."[118]

Similarly, the instruction concerning women found in 1 Timothy 2:11 ff. is part of a series of instructions for orderly worship. Donald Guthrie points out that there may have been local reasons for this prohibition of which we know nothing.[119] And here too we should note that there may be good reason to respect the "regulations and patterns of the non-Christian community in whose presence worship takes place."[120] In the Jewish synagogue, women were not permitted to speak and were to remain silent.[121] Therefore, not being offensive in Paul's day would mean not permitting a woman to teach. In fact such a situation would not have been tolerated at all. It is for this reason that I believe Jesus chose twelve men for disciples, that Paul gave the instructions he did in 1 Corinthians 14 and 1 Timothy 2. Such a practice would be quite consistent with the attitude of Jesus and Paul as discussed earlier—an attitude of self-sacrifice and voluntary subordination. Paul applied this attitude in other areas, for example, when he circumcised Timothy (Acts 16:3) even though he argued against making circumcision a requirement in the church, and when he advises abstinence from eating meat as a consideration to the weaker brother (1 Corinthians 8).[122]

It is unfortunate that the word "usurp" in the KJV translation of 1 Timothy 2:12 has been used as a blanket prohibition against women serving in various offices in the church. The Greek word here translated is *Authenteo,* meaning "to act of oneself, dominate."[123] The prohibition is against a woman forcing herself into some position of power, an action inappropriate for any Christian, man or woman. The reference to Creation, with Adam created first and Eve being deceived, is a further reminder to squelch any haughty spirit. The close of verse 15 is a reminder of the kind of life that becomes a Christian woman. Such a life will lead to the interdependence which was God's intention in the Garden.

4

CONCLUSION

In Ephesians 2:14-16, the Apostle Paul writes:

> For he [Christ] is our peace, who has made us both one,
> and has broken down the dividing wall of hostility, by
> abolishing in his flesh the law of commandments and ordi-
> nances, that he might create in himself one new man in
> place of two, so making peace, and might reconcile us both
> to God in one body through the cross, thereby bringing the
> hostility to an end.

This passage describes the essence of the church. It is
a people no longer separated by social conventions. It is
a people who now live by the Spirit of God, bound
together by His love, living in His peace, discovering
true fellowship with Him and with each other. "The
peoplehood called *Ekklesia* is different from other peo-
ples in its composition. It includes Jew and Gentile (not
simply two other groups, but two cultural types). It includes both masters and slaves and makes them brothers

54

and sisters 'not only in the spirit but also in the flesh' (Philemon v. 16). It includes men and women, replacing their hierarchical relationship in pagan society with mutual subordination (Ephesians 5:21). It shares money and bread and the gifts of the Spirit in a way that is a radical alternative to the authority structures of Gentile society. In all of these respects and more, the Christian community provides both a place to stand from which to say to the world something critically new and a place to keep testing and exercising the understanding of that critical message."[124]

With this understanding of the church in mind, an understanding basic to the perspective of this book, I want to make several observations. First, we need more critical discernment of the traditional teaching on the role of women in the church. Much of it reflects an attitude that might be called the "leaven of the Pharisees"—that is that the life of the people of God is still based on the "law of commandments and ordinances." However, the Apostle Paul points out that these have been abolished by Christ. Further, our traditional teaching reflects the thinking of society which does not follow Jesus in His self-giving love, but tries to maintain itself with coercive power. The Bible tells us the church is to be the body of Christ, having been transformed by the renewal of the mind (Romans 12:1, 2). It is to live out His will in this world. The life of this community is to be maintained by the gifts of the Spirit that Christ has given (Ephesians 4:4 ff.).

Second, we need to be discerning in our attitude toward the contemporary feminist movement. We ought to be supportive of attempts to get equal pay for equal work and equal opportunity in society. However, where the movement reflects the same attitude toward power that characterizes the society it protests, then we need to be prophetic. In the church we need not grapple for positions of power in order to change society for the better. The change has already happened. What is needed is for the church to be the church, living in the hope of the consummation yet to come.

My third observation concerns the family. I believe the problems Christian families are experiencing today (and that they experienced in the past) exist precisely because the teaching that has come to them from the church has reflected too much the thinking of the society around them in which they were trying to live. The traditional teaching about subjection and headship, as a model for husband/wife relationships, is not fundamentally different from the way in which society in general talks about them. It depends on a hierarchical structure that tries to maintain itself by force (either overt or covert) and manipulation while paying lip service to the meaning of love. Thus family life suffers from the same deficiencies which society suffers, the weakness of our own humanness, what the Bible calls the flesh.

Strengthening Christian families will only happen when we discover the meaning of church and understand relationships within the context of the church. Only as married men and women, who are Christian, discover that they are brothers and sisters in Christ before they are husbands and wives will they begin to find ways to overcome the problems confronting them from outside and inside their families. As Paul M. Lederach has said, "If we are to work in a significant way with biological families, we must begin with the spiritual family—the sons (and daughters) of God, the children of God, those who gather around Jesus Christ, who hear and obey His Word. For, as Jesus said, His Word is spirit and it is life (John 6:63). This family is open to the teaching and leading of the Holy Spirit."[125]

The spiritual family, the church, is not limited by the deficiencies of the larger society outside. Within the spiritual family, biological families can depend on the power of God's Spirit to govern their lives. As part of this power, families can discover that the congregation is a resource to help them on their way. Further, each biological family that is a part of the church will bring the principles that govern congregational life under the Spirit to bear in their individual homes. Only as these principles become a reality in each congregation, and from there to each family, will new vitality and life be found for family living. The principles I am refering to are those outlined in the Sermon on The Mount (Matthew 5, 6, 7) and in what has been called the "Rule of Christ" (Matthew 18:15 ff.) to name a few.

Guy Hershberger has described well what such a family would be like:

> The ideal here envisioned is that of a family where the worth and dignity of every member is recognized, and where every member shares, each according to his age and capacity to understand, in the common tasks of the family and in the formulation of its policies. In such a family husbands love their wives as their own bodies, and wives reciprocate with reverence and cooperation. Parents love their children, not provoking them to anger, but bringing them up in the discipline and instruction of the Lord. Such discipline in the home will be of the same firm but gentle character as that in the church as described in Matthew 18, where faults are frankly discussed between person and

57

person, and even before the whole council if need be, but where forgiveness is always extended, even unto seventy times seven. Such discipline is not punitive in character. It is a form of mutual burden bearing where children learn to reverence their elders because of their love, their wisdom, and the diligence with which they lead their children in finding the way in life which enables them to minister to the welfare of others and which brings to their own souls the deepest satisfactions which life can provide.[126]

Third we must also be sensitive to the single people in the church. Our congregational life at present leaves single men and women (particularly women) on the sidelines. Emotionally they are not part of the inner life of the congregation, even if they are given "something to do." We have failed to capture their gifts, because we accept without question the attitude of our society which gives preeminence to marriage (this may be more true at certain times than others, but the general attitude in society is that everyone ought to marry sometime). This problem is enhanced in our midst by the traditional teaching of subjection and headship which presupposes marriage.[127] By giving preeminence to marriage, we have missed important biblical teaching about those who have made themselves "eunuchs" (symbolic of being unmarried) for the kingdom's sake (Matthew 19:12).

The church needs to hear again the words of Jesus, "Whoever does the will of God is my brother, and sister, and mother" (Mark 3:35).[128] We need to hear again the words of Paul that it is good to remain unmarried and not hampered by the necessities of married life in the service of the Lord.[129] In the church there is no favored group of people—not even the married—only brothers and sisters in Christ, each with a gift or gifts necessary for the function and well-being of their particular congregation. In the church everyone, whether married or single, can find (or should find) strength and meaning for living in the Spirit, in mutual subordination as the love of God is shed abroad in their hearts. Thus the church is truly a community of believers and not just a community of the married.

Reflecting on the Daytons' article, "Women as Preachers: Evangelical Precedents" (see footnote 105), it is significant that there has always been less resistance toward women playing a major role in congregational life among the believers' churches than in the major Protestant denominations with their roots in Reformed or Lutheran traditions. In their early years in America, the believers' churches showed little resistence to women preaching, defending this practice Biblically. Later years evidence a decline and greater resistence to the practice. In light of their history, which is a greater accommodation to "the world" for the believers' churches? Allowing women a larger role in the congregation (even preaching) based on the gifting of the Holy Spirit, or resisting such a move?

My fourth observation concerns the ordination of women. Based on the kind of definition of the church that I have found in the Bible and I have attempted to outline in this book, I see no reason why women cannot be admitted to the preaching ministry. Within the Anabaptist/Mennonite tradition, we understand the Bible to teach that the church is a "community." To be precise, we call it the "community of the Spirit." We understand the preaching/teaching ministry as one of the gifts of the Spirit given for the welfare of the community.[130] It is one gift among many, none of which supersedes the other.

Much of the thinking that opposes admitting women to the preaching ministry has its roots in a theology which has a hierarchical view of the church. In such a theology, the minister stands in a special relation to God by virtue of his ordination and thus possesses a special authority as God's spokesman. Scripture, it is said, bars woman from this office. By order of creation, Adam was created first and therefore subject to God, while woman is subject to the man. Further, it is said that woman was placed under man's authority after the Fall. Therefore, she cannot be admitted to the preaching ministry, since that would place her in authority over man.

Those of us in the Anabaptist/Mennonite and believers' church tradition need to be careful how we borrow from the hierarchical view lest we find ourselves in contradiction with what we believe the Bible teaches about the nature of the church. (At this point it is not my intention to say which view is biblical or unbiblical, or to pass judgment on either. I am only attempting to make a point about consistency of conviction.) We do not hold to a hierarchical view of the church. For us it is more a family that one enters at conversion by the regenerating power of the Holy Spirit. Life is lived in this family by the power of the Spirit, who gives to each His gifts as He wills for the well-being of the family. Since we all share equally in the Holy Spirit, who makes us one (Ephesians 4:4 ff., Romans 12:4), and the church, born of the Spirit, is a return to a life of interdependency between the members and dependency on God which was intended in the Garden, I see no reason to believe that women will not be given the gift to preach as well as men. Not that we have achieved interdependency perfectly here, but rather as God gives us His strength we keep moving toward the hope set before us in joyful anticipation of its coming.

When anyone is united to Christ, there is a new world; the old order has gone, and a new order has already begun.
—2 Corinthians 5:17, NEB

Therefore, let the church be the church!

APPENDIX

A Brief Discussion of the "Chain of Command"

There are those who see in 1 Corinthians 11:3 and in Ephesians 5:23 a hierarchy of authority whereby the wife is under the husband in a kind of "chain of command," therefore subject to his authority. In times past, physical, intellectual, and even spiritual inferiority were thought to be implied in these verses and this was used to inforce a wife's total subjection to her husband. Today, only a functional subjection is taught. The wife is not said to be inferior to her husband, only that her role is to be his "helper." Therefore, she is to abide by his decision whether at home, in the church, or in general public. She may share her thoughts, but in all cases must abide by the husband's final decision. This is the will of God, who from creation, appointed the husband as "head" of the wife.

A weakness in this line of thought is that "none of the relationships mentioned in (1 Corinthians 11:3) . . . is exactly the same as the others."[131] The wife is not subject to the husband in the same way Christ was to God the Father. There is no way that a husband and wife can have that close a relationship due to our own humanity. Nor is the wife subject to her husband in the exact same way that we expect Christian men and women to be subject to Christ as their "head." There may well be certain times, when due to her commitment to Christ, the Christian wife may have to act contrary to the wishes of her husband just as the Christian husband may need to act contrary to the wishes of his wife (cf. Acts 4:19, 5:29). We can look at Peter's allusion to Sarah and Abraham (1 Peter 3:6) as an illustration. Peter calls upon Christian wives to follow Sarah in their respect for their husbands. But understanding that, none of us expects a Christian wife to go and live with another man on command of her husband as Sarah did on two occasions (Genesis 12:10 ff.; 20:2 ff.). There is no reason to believe that Peter had these two occasions in mind, but they do serve to illustrate my point. Showing due respect is one thing. But blind obedience to a fallible human being is folly and can result in disobedience to God as Peter himself recognized in the references to Acts cited above. One cannot logically build a military type chain of command out of these verses. The lines of relationship are not the same.

A further problem with this view is that the chain of command presupposes the marriage relationship—so much so that it cannot be applied to all human situations. For example, to whom is the single woman with no living male relatives to be subject? And if she does have a living uncle or brother, how does one define her subjection? How is she to be functionally subordinate to them? And if her father is still living, how does an adult single woman relate to him? In Western cultures at least, with its nuclear family structure, there is no practical way the chain of command is relevent to the single woman. It appears to impose an alien structure on these passages of the Apostle Paul, without relating them to the rest of his writings and the rest of the Scriptures.

We find some help in understanding these passages if we look at the words "man" and "woman" in 1 Corinthians 11:3. Most commentators agree that Paul has the husband/wife relationship in mind here. Bill Detweiler summarizes the evidence well: "The Greek words here used for 'man' and 'woman' are the common Greek words *Aneer* and *Gunee*. In the New Testament *Aneer* is 50 times translated "husband" and 156 times translated as 'man." *Gunee* is translated 'wife' 92 times, and 'woman' 129 times. The most often used word for 'man' is *Anthropos,* which is never translated 'husband' but is consistently translated 'man' (in more than 550 usages). It is perhaps noteworthy that in this Corinthian passage Paul used the word *Aneer* rather than *Anthropos,* because if he meant specifically to use the term 'husband' *Aneer* was the only word he could use. And if he meant specifically to use the word 'wife,' *Gunee* was the only word at his disposal. As mentioned earlier, the Greek words *Aneer* and *Gunee* are the words Paul uses in Ephesians 5:23 when he speaks specifically of the husband-wife relationship."[132]

This supports my contention that Paul's intention was to speak to the husband/wife relationship specifically, and that his instructions were practical applications of what it would mean in that situation (whatever it might be) for them to follow through on their commitment to "be subject to one another out of reverence for Christ" (Ephesians 5:21). Subjection then was a matter of nonresistance for the Christian wives. And to define it, we ought to search such passages as Romans 12:3 ff.; Colossians 3:12 ff. (noting particulary v. 17), and 1 John 3:11 f.; 4:7 ff. All of these passages speak of the Christian life as one of love and self-sacrifice. Such a life is applicable to all men and women, married or single, for this is the very life of Christ to which we are called.

NOTES

1. C. Norman Kraus, *The Community of the Spirit* (Grand Rapids: Eerdmans, 1974), p. 9. For further reading on the church from this perspective, see H. S. Bender, *These Are My People* (Scottdale: Herald Press, 1962) and John Driver, *Community and Commitment* (Scottdale: Herald Press, 1976). For this concept in Anabaptist/ Mennonite theology, see Robert Friedmann, *The Theology of Anabaptism* (Scottdale: Herald Press, 1973).

2. Kraus, p. 9.

3. *Ibid.,* pp. 13-14.

4. *Ibid.,* p. 15.

5. *Ibid.,* pp. 27-28.

6. *Ibid.,* p. 55.

7. *Ibid.*

8. *Ibid.,* pp. 32-33.

9. *Ibid.*

10. Guy F. Hershberger, *The Way of the Cross in Human Relations* (Scottdale: Herald Press, 1958), p. 20. While Hershberger's book deals mainly with international relations, and a Christian's relationship to those situations, I believe the insight that he brings is applicable to all human relationships, individual or corporate. He does this himself near the back of the book where he discusses personal relations. His view of the "order of creation" as having to do with justice and righteousness rooted in the holiness of God is most insightful and needed.

11. *Ibid.*

12. For a survey of the various interpretations in past and present Jewish and Christian teachings, see Lois Gunden Clemens, *Woman Liberated* (Scottdale: Herald Press, 1971), pp. 13-24. Also, Paul K.

Jewett, *Man as Male and Female* (Grand Rapids: Eerdmans, 1975), pp. 49-94.

13. Dorothy Yoder Nyce, "Woman: In God's Plan and Man's World," Part I, *Gospel Herald,* August 7, 1973, p. 606.

14. Nyce quoting Helmut Thielicke, *Ibid.*

15. Nor is there any reason to believe that the sexual act was unknown to them before they sinned, or that it was the "original sin." Verse 28 would imply otherwise.

16. Jewett, p. 36

17. For a complete discussion of this point, see pp. 33-40 in Jewett. I will discuss briefly the meaning of the "image of God" and its relationship to human sexuality in the following pages.

18. See Jewett, pp. 61-86 for illustrations. Also Hershberger, pp. 354-355 has some illustrations of the prevailing attitude toward women from late 19th-century America.

19. Hershberger, p. 348.

20. Clemens, pp. 13 ff. The word "generic" means of a kind or class.

21. *Ibid.*, p. 14.

22. Exodus 18:4.

23. Psalms 33:20; 115:9, 10, 11.

24. James Strong, *The Exhaustive Concordance of the Bible* (New York/Nashville: Abingdon, 1890), see p. 86, word number 5828 in the accompanying Hebrew dictionary.

25. Clemens, p. 14.

26. Richard J. Mouw, *Politics and the Biblical Drama* (Grand Rapids: Eerdmans, 1976), pp. 23 ff.

27. *Ibid.*, p. 24.

28. Hershberger, p. 12.

29. The Westminster Shorter Catechism of 1647. Recorded by Philip Schaff, *The Creeds of Christendom,* Vol. III (Grand Rapids: Baker Book House, 1966), pp. 677-678.

30. Mouw, p. 24.

31. *Ibid.*

32. Mouw quoting Barth, *Ibid.,* p. 25.

33. See Jewett, pp. 33-40

34. Mouw, p. 26.

35. Mouw, p. 27.

36. *Ibid.*

37. *Ibid.*, p. 28.

38. Clemens, p. 14.

39. Hershberger, p. 348.

40. By "many different levels of human relationship," I mean as

friends, parent/child, husband/wife, employer/employee, etc. Each learning from the other, thus giving a deeper understanding of themselves, others, and God.

41. Positive social relationships are important for our understanding of ourselves. Since each of us occupies different points in space and time, each of our perspectives on life can be enriched by others' perspectives on life. Note, too, that such encounters will enhance our understanding of God, since we can share from their unique encounter with God.

42. Sherwin Bailey, *Sexual Ethics* (New York: Macmillan, 1963), p. 81.

43. *Ibid.*

44. *Ibid.*, p. 80.

45. *Ibid.*

46. *Ibid.*, pp. 80-81.

47. *Ibid.*, p. 81.

48. See p. 11 above.

49. Hershberger, pp. 348-349.

50. For excellent help in interpreting this account, see J. C. Wenger, *Introduction to Theology* (Scottdale: Herald Press, 1954), pp. 87-90; and C. K. Lehman, *Biblical Theology* (Scottdale: Herald Press, 1971), Vol. I, pp. 58-66.

51. Vernard Eller, *King Jesus' Manual of Arms for the 'Armless* (Nashville: Abingdon, 1973), p. 21.

52. See Jewett, pp. 61-86 for illustrations and discussions of this argument.

53. Note Psalm 103:12; Jeremiah 3:12 ff; 31:34; Romans 1:16; 6:23 to name only a few. There are those who would say that disease and death and the "curse" of the soil entered human experience at the Fall, and God has not revoked them with the forgiveness of sin. Therefore, woman must still be under the restriction of Genesis 3. The problem is that there is always the tendency to interpret disease, death, and the like as punishment. A better way of viewing these things might be to see them entering as a consequence of humanity's choice, rather than as a punitive measure by God. Further, the New Testament forgiveness of sin is coupled with victory over disease and death and an anticipation of a restoration of the earth. See Romans 8:19 ff. Note also John's vision of the new heaven and new earth in Revelation. In Jesus' ministry, miracles of healing are coupled with forgiveness of sin (i.e., Mark 2:9). He gave His disciples power over disease (Luke 10). The early church practiced healing in the name of Jesus and anointed the sick (James 5:13 ff), evidence that they believed that Jesus overcame disease and death at the cross as well as

conquering sin. Not that there is no disease or death for Christians, but in the midst of suffering, we live out Jesus' life in the power of His Spirit looking for the blessed hope. (Note Romans 8:23).

54. Dorothy Yoder Nyce, "Woman: In God's Plan and Man's World," Part II, *Gospel Herald,* August 14, 1973, p. 622.

55. Robert Hartzler, "Making Up Our Minds About Women," *Christian Living,* July 1976, p. 26.

'56. I consulted the King James Version, the Revised Standard Version, Today's English Version, and *The Jerusalem Bible.*

57. Nyce, Part II. p. 622.

58. For illustrations of the belief that women are inferior and/or inherently evil, see Jewett, pp. 149-162. For another interesting illustration taken from church history, see David Augsburger, *Cherishable: Love and Marriage* (Scottdale: Herald Press, 1971), p. 43.

59. Clemens, p. 21.

60. Jewett, pp. 86-94. It should not surprise us that these are recorded in the Bible. The Bible gives us a picture of human life as it is, revealing God's will over against human existence. Such exposure is an indicator of how far human civilization of any time period is from the will of God.

61. *Ibid.,* p. 91.

62. *Ibid.,* p. 87.

63. In spite of this we will see in a moment how large a part women did play.

64. Nyce, Part II, p. 621.

65. That sin abuses the law is the crux of Paul's argument in Romans 7.

66. The preceeding illustrations are noted by Clemens, pp. 91-93.

67. Nyce, Part II, p. 622.

68. See Joachim Jeremias, *Jerusalem in the Time of Jesus* (Philadelphia: Fortress Press, 1975), pp. 359-376.

69. However, note Jesus' teaching on divorce and remarriage (Matthew 19:1-12 and parallels). This incident did "sharply contrast" with the custom of the time. But in the main, Jesus' attitude is seen largely in His actions rather than summarized in any specific teaching about women.

70. Jewett, p. 94.

71. Clemens, pp. 95-96. For documentation and illustrations of the Jewish religious leaders' restrictions concerning women, see Jeremias, p. 360, paragraph 2.

72. For the following summary of Jesus' encounter with women, I give credit to Daniel Yutzy who first made me aware of these examples in a chapel address, "The Role of Women in the Church Alive,"

given at Eastern Mennonite College, January 1974. His address is a background for my thoughts in this section, but any conclusions are my own.

73. Because of the sexual overtones our society has given to the word "intimate," I will need to define it. I am using the word here in the same way. Yutzy did in his address to mean "warm, close, personal, fellowship."

74. Compare Matthew 26:6-13 and Mark 14:3-9. Also, John 12:1-8 where Mary, Lazarus' sister, wipes Jesus feet. Jewett, pp. 99-100, gives a most insightful comment on this passage, pointing out the social implications of Martha serving a table of all men (a job done usually by male free servants or slaves) and of Mary's behavior, especially letting her hair down in the presence of men (at that time deemed highly immodest).

75. It is interesting to note that the last verses in Leviticus 15 which apply to men are often overlooked.

76. There are Old Testament passages where God refers to Himself in feminine terms: Isaiah 49:15 or Deuteronomy 32:18 where the imagery in the Hebrew is a woman giving birth. In the KJV this is not clear. The RSV is closer to the true meaning of the Hebrew. *The Jerusalem Bible* obscures the meaning altogether by using "fatherhood" for the second verb in the sentence. "It imposes male imagery on female usage," according to Jewett, page 167, footnote 136, which includes a fuller discussion of this verse. Another example of obscuring references to female imagery in the English translation is Psalms 68:11. The KJV and the RSV translations are both obscure in this case. The *Pulpit Commentary* says this verse literally reads, "great was the company of the women that heralded it." *Pulpit Commentary* (Chicago, Wilcox & Follett Co.), Vol. 18: Psalms, Vol. II, p. 44. There is also an interesting reference to Jeremiah 31:22, especially in light of the debate surrounding authority of men over women. For a more complete discussion of feminine terms used to refer to God, see Phyllis Trible's article, "God, Nature of, in the O.T.", Interpreter's Dictionary of the Bible, (Abingdon: Nashville, 1976), Supplimentary Volume, pp. 368-369.

77. Jewett, p. 91.

78. Clemens, p. 104.

79. M. J. Shroyer, "Aquila and Priscilla," *The Interpreter's Dictionary of the Bible,* George Arthur Buttrick, ed., Vol. I, p. 176.

80. J. B. Smith, *Greek-English Concordance* (Scottdale: Herald Press, 1955), p. 84.

81. Clemens, p. 105.

82. Charles Caldwell Ryrie, *The Role of Women in the Church*

(Chicago: Moody Press, 1970), p. 89.

83. Clemens, p. 104.

84. *Ibid.*, p. 105.

85. *Ibid.*, pp. 105-106.

86. *Ibid.*

87. *Women in the Church* a study document prepared by the Mennonite Board of Congregational Ministries in cooperation with the Women's Missionary and Service Commission of the Mennonite Church (1973), p. 10.

88. Esther K. Augsburger, WMSC *Devotional Guide for 1975-1976.* General Executive Committee, Women's Missionary and Service Commission of the Mennonite Church.

89. For the complete story, see Mary Lou Cummings article, "The History Written in Pencil," *The Mennonite,* January 18, 1977, pp. 34 ff.

90. For some illustrations, see *The Complete Writings of Menno Simons,* J. C. Wenger, Trans. (Scottdale: Herald Press, 1956). Note Menno's instructions to women in the article, "True Christian Faith," p. 383.

91. Jewett, pp. 111-119.

92. Robin Scroggs, "Paul: Chauvenist or Liberationist?" *Christian Century,* March 15, 1972.

93. Jewett, p. 114.

94. For example see Aland, *et. al., Greek New Testament* (New York: American Bible Society, 1966), p. 611.

95. John H. Yoder, *Politics of Jesus* (Grand Rapids: Eerdmans, 1972), p. 177, footnote 24.

96. For example note the following:

   a. Elizabeth Elliot Leitch, "Why I Oppose the Ordination of Women," *Christianity Today* June 6, 1975, p. 12 ff. Or her article, "Liberation—Christian Style," *The Presbyterian Journal,* May 25, 1977, pp. 7 ff.

   b. C. S. Lewis, *Mere Christianity* (New York: Macmillan, 1967), pp. 102-103.

   c. Marabel Morgan, *The Total Woman* (Old Tappan: Revell, 1975). Note that while Morgan espouses subjection of wives in the traditional sense, she turns it into a way of manipulating the husband. She has the appearance of subjection, but in fact advocates coercion (however mild). For a most insightful article see, "The Total Woman," Abraham and Dorothy Schmitt, *Christian Living,* December 1975, pp, 10-14.

97. For example:

   a. Daniel Kauffman, ed., *Doctrines of the Bible* (Scottdale: Mennonite Publishing House, 1949), p. 412.

b. John Gill, *Body of Divinity* (Atlanta: Turner Lassetter, 1965).

c. Such Commentaries as the *Pulpit Commentary, The Tyndale New Testament,* Charles Hodge, John Calvin, John Eadie.

98. For two examples, see Kauffman, p. 412; Lewis, pp. 102-103.

99. For three examples, see H. Berkhof, *Christ and the Powers,* J. H. Yoder, Trans. (Scottdale: Herald Press, 1962). Also, Yoder, pp. 135 ff. And more recently, Mouw, pp. 85 ff. Mouw quotes Berkhof quite extensively and in the footnote on p. 86 lists some other important sources.

100. In Romans 8:19-23, the Apostle Paul implies the "fallenness" of nature. See foonote 54 above.

101. Verse 21 is variously located in this chapter by translators. The RSV, *The Jerusalem Bible,* and the Berkeley Version place it with the paragraph dealing with man/woman relationships. The Second Edition Greek New Testament of the American Bible Society, the KJV, and Williams place it with the paragraph beginning with verse 15. The TEV and the NEB set verse 21 as a paragraph by itself between the paragraphs of 15 ff. and 22 ff. including it however under the section heading "Wives and Husbands." The question of where verse 21 belongs has little bearing upon the argument I am about to make. The apostle is calling upon the Ephesian Christians to follow Christ in all their relationships with one another—whether that be in the church as brothers and sisters in Christ or in the home as husbands and wives.

102. Nolan B. Harmon, ed., *The Interpreter's Bible,* Vol. X (New York-Nashville: Abingdon Press), p. 719.

103. Compare Matthew 20:20 ff.; Mark 10:35 ff.; John 13:3-16.

104. This thought was suggested by Myron Augsburger in "Anabaptist Vision," an address given at Ministers' Week, Eastern Mennonite College, January 1975 (transcribed).

105. The issues of women's rights and slavery (civil rights today) have always gone hand in hand in this country. The struggle for women's liberation is not new. Women in the abolitionist movement of the nineteenth century worked for women's suffrage. Women in the civil rights and anti-war movements of the 1960s are now at work in the women's liberation movement. Further, it is interesting to ponder the close parallels between the sermons teaching female subjection as an "order of creation" and the sermons of the nineteeth century that taught slavery for the black people as an "order of creation." For a discussion of the rise of revivalism and the abolition of slavery, see Dr. Timothy L. Smith, *Revivalism and Social Reform: American Protestantism on the Eve of the Civil War* (Gloucester: Peter

Smith, 1976), pp. 178-224. And on the same movement's effect on the suffragette cause and ordination of women, see Donald W. and Lucille Sider Dayton's article, "Women as Preachers: Evangelical Precedents," *Christianity Today,* May 23, 1975, pp. 4-7. Also, Sharon Gallager's article, "The Second-Rate Rib," *Sojourners,* January 1977, Supplimental Issue, "The Seed's of the Kingdom," pp. 60 ff. See also, Catherine Booth's *"Female Ministry"* (New York: The Salvation Army, 1975), for an early defense of a women's right to preach.

106. Yoder, p. 177, footnote 24.

107. In light of the foregoing discussion, I do not see how as Mennonites we can maintain our peace position and still teach subjection and headship as we have done in the past and in some cases still do. No matter how a person may attempt to qualify the language by speaking of the need to love while still being "head," the implied maintenance of a position of power remains from which one can impose his will on another against her will. That is not the life of servanthood as we see it in Jesus, who came as one who serves. The fact that we have been able to teach subjection and headship as we have, and still maintain a stance as a Peace Church, is evidence of how fragmented and isolated an understanding and application of the Scriptures many of us have. As evidence for my statement, I point the reader to Hershberger, p. 355 ff., especially of his report of J. Howard Kauffman's survey done in 1957. The crux of what Hershberger says is that Mennonites in this century have not learned to apply the "way of the cross" in their immediate families.

108. Yoder, p. 192.

109. See the Appendix for a discussion of Paul's use of the word "head" and the significance of the words "man" and "woman" used in this passage.

110. See Romans 12:3, 10.

111. Clemens, p. 132.

112. The *Tyndale New Testament Commentaries,* R. V. G. Tasker, general editor (Grand Rapids: Eerdmans, 1972), Vol. 7: *I Corinthians, An Introduction and Commentary* by Leon Morris, p. 153.

113. See Romans 12:4 ff.; 1 Corinthians 12:12 ff.

114. Perhaps greater consistency with this passage would be to adopt the wedding band as a symbol of respect in marriage. As used in our culture, the wedding band carries the same meaning as the veiling did in Corinth.

115. See examples in page 27 of this study.

116. Clemens, pp. 133-134 and 135-136.

117. See page 44 in this book.

118. Nyce, "Women: In God's Plan and Man's World," Part III, *Gospel Herald,* August 21, 1973, p. 637. (Parentheses mine.)

119. The *Tyndale New Testament Commentaries,* R. V. G. Tasker, general editor (Grand Rapids: Eerdmans, 1972), Vol. 14: *The Pastoral Epistles, An Introduction and Commentary* by Donald Guthrie, p. 76.

120. See page 51 of this book.

121. See Jeremias, pp. 373-375 and further references in Guthrie, p. 76.

122. Note on this point 1 Corinthians 7:17 ff. where Paul, in discussing the particular advantages and disadvantages of being married or unmarried in serving the Lord, says, "Every one should remain in the state in which he was called" (v. 20). In v. 17, he calls such conditions states which the Lord has assigned whether it be a state of circumcision or uncircumcision (v. 18), slavery (v. 23), being single or married (v. 25). The apparent meaning is, whatever condition you were in when God called you, there serve the Lord.

123. Strong, see p. 17, word number 831, of the accompanying Greek Dictionary.

124. John H. Yoder, "The Biblical Mandate," *Sojourners,* January 1977, Supplimental Issue, "Seeds of the Kingdom," p. 16.

125. Paul M. Lederach, *The Spiritual Family and the Biological Family* (Scottdale: Herald Press, 1973), Focal Pamphlet No. 24, pp. 16-17. The parenthesis, "(and daughters)," is my addition.

126. Hershberger, p. 359. See also my article, "Family Life in the Kingdom of God," *Gospel Herald,* January 13, 1976, pp. 20-22.

127. See the appendix for further discussion of this point.

128. Compare Matthew 12:46-50; Luke 8:19-21.

129. See 1 Corinthians 7 and footnote 122 of this study.

130. See 1 Corinthians 12 and Ephesians 4. and any parallels. Also review the discussion of the church at the beginning of this study.

131. Morris, *Commentary on 1 Corinthians,* p. 151.

132. Bill Detweiler, *Another Look at 1 Corinthians 11:2-16* (Privately printed, 1970), p. 19. Used by permission. Prepared for a congregational study at the Kidron Mennonite Church, Kidron, Ohio.

BIBLIOGRAPHY

General Reference Works

Augsburger, David W. *Cherishable: Love and Marriage.* Scottdale: Herald Press, 1971.

Augsburger, Esther K. *Devotional Guide, 1975-1976.* Elkhart: Women's Missionary and Service Commission of the Mennonite Church.

Bailey, Sherwin, *Sexual Ethics: A Christian View.* New York: Macmillan, 1963.

Bender, H. S. *These Are My People.* Scottdale: Herald Press, 1962.

Berkhof, H. *Christ and the Powers.* Scottdale: Herald Press, 1962.

Booth Catherine. *Female Ministry.* New York: The Salvation Army, 1975.

Clemens, Lois G. *Woman Liberated.* Scottdale: Herald Press, 1971

Detweiler, Bill. *Another Look at 1 Corinthians 11:2-16.* Privately printed, 1970.

Driver, John. *Community and Commitment.* Scottdale: Herald Press, 1976.

Eller, Vernard. *King Jesus' Manual of Arms for the 'Armless.* New York, Nashville: Abingdon, 1973.

Friedmann, Robert. *The Theology of Anabaptism.* Scottdale: Herald Press, 1973.

Gill, John. *Body of Divinity.* Atlanta: Turner Lassetter, 1965.

Hershberger, Guy F. *The Way of the Cross in Human Relations.* Scottdale: Herald Press, 1958.

Jeremias, Joachim. *Jerusalem in the Time of Jesus.* Philadelphia: Fortress Press, 1975.

Jewett, Paul K. *Man as Male and Female.* Grand Rapids: Eerdmans, 1974.

75

Kauffman, Daniel (ed.). *Doctrines of the Bible*. Scottdale: Mennonite Publishing House, 1928.

Kraus, C. Norman. *The Community of the Spirit*. Grand Rapids: Eerdmans, 1974.

Lederach, Paul M. *The Spiritual Family and the Biological Family*. Focal Pamphlet No. 24. Scottdale: Herald Press, 1973.

Lehman, C. K. *Biblical Theology: Old Testament*. Scottdale: Herald Press, 1971.

Lewis, C. S. *Mere Christianity*. New York: Macmillan, 1960.

Morgan, Marabel. *The Total Woman*. Old Tappan: Revell, 1973.

Mouw, Richard J. *Politics and the Biblical Drama*. Grand Rapids: Eerdmans, 1976.

Ryrie, Charles Caldwell. *The Role of Women in the Church*. Chicago: Moody Press, 1955.

Schaff, Philip. *The Creeds of Christendom*, Vol. III. Grand Rapids: Baker, 1966.

Smith, Timothy L. *Revivalism and Social Reform: Protestantism on the Eve of the Civil War*. Gloucester: Peter Smith, 1976.

Wenger, J. C. (Trans.). *The Complete Writings of Menno Simons*. Scottdale: Herald Press, 1956.

Wenger, J. C. *Introduction to Theology*. Scottdale: Herald Press, 1954.

Women in the Church. A study document prepared by the Mennonite Board of Congregational Ministries in cooperation with the Women's Missionary and Service Commission of the Mennonite Church.

Yoder, John H. *The Politics of Jesus*. Grand Rapids: Eerdmans, 1972.

Bible Commentaries

Calvin, John. *Calvin's Commentaries*, Vols. 1, 11, 12. Grand Rapids: Associated Publishers and Authors.

Eadie, John. *Colossians*. Minneapolis: James and Klock Christian Publishing Company, 1977 (reprint).

Hodge, Charles. *1 Corinthians and Ephesians*. London: The Banner of Truth Trust, 1964.

Harmon, Nolan B. (ed.). *The Interpreter's Bible*, Vol. X. New York and Nashville: Abingdon Press, 1953.

Spence, H. D. M., *et. al.* (eds.). *The Pulpit Commentary*, Vols. 1, 44, 46, 47. Chicago: Wilcox & Follett.

Tasker, R. V. G. (general editor). *Tyndale New Testament Commentaries*, Vols. 7, 14. Grand Rapids: Eerdmans, 1972.

Bible Dictionaries and Concordances

Buttrick, George A. (ed.). *Interpreter's Dictionary of the Bible,* Vol. 1. New York and Nashville: Abingdon Press, 1962.

Crim, Keith (General ed.) *Interpreter's Dictionary of the Bible, Supplimentary Volume,* Nashville: Abingdon Press, 1976.

Smith, J. B. *Greek-English Concordance.* Scottdale: Herald Press, 1955.

Strong, James. *The Exhaustive Concordance of the Bible.* New York and Nashville: Abingdon Press, 1890.

Articles and Periodicals

Collins, Sheila D. "Toward a Feminist Theology," *Christian Century,* August 2, 1972.

Cummings, Mary Lou. "The History Written in Pencil," *The Mennonite,* January 18, 1977.

Dayton, Donald W., and Lucille Sider. "Women as Preachers: Evangelical Precedents," *Christianity Today,* May 23, 1975.

Elliot, Elisabeth. "Why I Oppose the Ordination of Women," *Christianity Today,* June 6, 1975.

Gallager, Sharon. "The Second-Rate Rib," *Sojourners,* Supplimentary Issue: "The Seeds of the Kingdom," January, 1977.

Leitch, Elisabeth Elliot. "Liberation—Christian Style," *The Presbyterian Journal,* May 25, 1977.

Hartzler, Robert. "Making Up Our Minds About Women," *Christian Living,* July 1976.

Kuhns, Dennis R. "Family Life in the Kingdom of God," *Gospel Herald,* January 13, 1976.

Nyce, Dorothy Yoder. "Women: God's Plan and Man's World," 3-Part series, *Gospel Herald,* August 7, 14, 21, 1973.

Schmitt, Abraham and Dorothy. "The Total Woman," *Christian Living,* December 1975.

Scroggs, Robin. "Paul: Chauvenist or Liberationist?" *Christian Century,* March 15, 1972.

Yoder, John H. "The Biblical Mandate," *Sojourners,* Supplementary Issue: "The Seeds of the Kingdom," January 1977.

Transcribed Material

Augsburger, Myron S. "Anabaptist Vision." Opening address given at Eastern Mennonite College, Ministers' Week, January 20, 1975 (tape recorded).

Yutzy, Daniel. "The Role of Women in the Church Alive." Chapel address given at Eastern Mennonite College, January 24, 1974 (tape recorded).

Biblical Translations

Aland, Kurt, *et. al. The Greek New Testament.* Second Edition. New York: American Bible Society, 1966, 1968.

Jones, Alexander, General Editor. *The Jerusalem Bible.* Garden City: Doubleday, 1966.

Lawson, J. Gilchrist. *The Marked Chain-Reference Bible: Being the King James or Authorized Version of the Old and New Testament.* Grand Rapids: Zondervan, 1963.

New English Bible: New Testament. Oxford/Cambridge: Oxford University Press, Cambridge University Press, 1961.

Revised Standard Version. Division of Christian Education of the National Council of the Churches of Christ in the United States of America, 1946, 1952.

Today's English Version. New York: American Bible Society, 1976.

Verkuyl, Gerrit. *Berkeley Version of the New Testament.* Grand Rapids: Zondervan, 1945.

Williams, Charles B. *The New Testament: A Translation in the Language of the People.* Chicago: Moody Press.

THE FOCAL PAMPHLET SERIES

1. *Intregration! Who's Prejudiced?* by C. Norman Kraus, (1958).
2. *The Church and the Community,* by J. Lawrence Burkholder (1958).
3. *The Ecumenical Movement and the Faithful Church,* by John H. Yoder (1959).
4. *Biblical Revelation and Inspiration,* by Harold S. Bender (1959).
5. *As You Go,* by John H. Yoder (1961). OP
6. *The Christian Calling,* by Virgil Vogt (1961). OP
7. *The Price of Church Unity,* by Harold E. Bauman (1962).
8. *Television: Friend or Foe?* by Henry Weaver (1962). OP
9. *Brotherhood and Schism,* by Calvin Redekop (1963).
10. *The Call to Preach,* by Clayton Beyler (1963). OP
11. *The Church Functions with Purpose,* by Calvin Redekop (1967).
12. *Let's Talk About Extremism,* by Edgar Metzler (1968).
13. *Helping Developing Countries,* by Carl Kreider (1968). OP
14. *The Christian Stance in a Revolutionary Age,* by Donald R. Jacobs (1968).
15. *Pacifism and Biblical Nonresistance,* by J. C. Wenger (1968).

16. *Evangelicalism and Social Responsibility,* by Vernon C. Grounds (1969).

17. *World Hunger: Reality and Challenge,* by C. Franklin Bishop (1969).

18. *The Problems of Nationalism in Church-State Relationships,* by James E. Wood, Jr. (1969).

19. *Change and the Church,* by Paul N. Kraybill (1970).

20. *The City: What Is It Really Like?* by Vern Miller (1970).

21. *Ecology of the Airwaves,* by LeRoy E. Kennel (1971)

22. *Demons,* by Donald R. Jacobs (1972).

23. *Making Political Decisions,* by John R. Redekop (1972).

24. *The Spiritual Family and the Biological Family,* by Paul M. Lederach (1973).

25. *Theology: White, Black, or Christian?* by Warner Jackson (1974).

26. *Release to Those in Prison,* by William Klassen (1977).

27. *Mennonite Education: Issues, Facts, and Changes,* by Donald B. Kraybill (1978).

28. *Women in the Church,* by Dennis R. Kuhns (1978).